JAMES VALENTINE
FLORIDA
IMAGES OF THE LANDSCAPE

PHOTOGRAPHY BY JAMES VALENTINE

WESTCLIFFE PUBLISHERS, INC. ENGLEWOOD, COLORADO

CONTENTS

International Standard Book Number: ISBN: 0-942394-59-3
Library of Congress Catalogue Card Number: 87-051501
Copyright, Photographs and Text: James Valentine, 1988
Editor: John Fielder
Assistant Editors: Scott Lankford, Margaret Terrell Morse
Production Manager: Mary Jo Lawrence
Typographer: Dianne J. Borneman
Printed In Singapore By Tien Wah Press
Published By Westcliffe Publishers
2650 South Zuni Street
Englewood, Colorado 80110

Bibliography

[The source is followed by the page number in this book on which the quotation appears.]

Audubon, John James: from *Audubon, By Himself*. Edited by Alice Ford. New York: The Natural History Press, 1969. Reprinted by permission of Doubleday Subrights: 78.

Audubon, John James: from *Audubon's America* by Donald Culross Peattie. Copyright © 1940 by Donald Culross Peattie. Copyright © renewed 1968 by Louise Redfield Peattie. Reprinted by permission of Houghton Mifflin Company: 158.

Bartram, William: from *Travels*. New York: Viking Penguin Inc., 1988. Reprinted by permission of Viking Penguin Inc.: 18, 22, 34, 42, 70, 106.

Carr, Archie: from *THE AMERICAN WILDERNESS/The Everglades* by Archie Carr and the Editors of Time-Life Books, copyright © 1973 Time-Life Books, Inc.: 98, 112, 120, 134, 154.

Carson, Rachel: from *Silent Spring* by Rachel Carson. Copyright © 1962 by Rachel L. Carson. Reprinted by permission of Houghton Mifflin Company: 38, 40.

Douglas, Marjory Stoneman: from *The Everglades: River of Grass*. Coconut Grove, Florida: Hurricane House Publishers, Inc., 1947. Copyright © 1947 by Marjory Stoneman Douglas. Reprinted by permission of the author: 122, 126, 130.

Muir, John A.: from *A Thousand Mile Walk to The Gulf* by John Muir. Copyright © 1916 by Houghton Mifflin Company. Copyright renewed © 1944 by Ellen Muir Funk. Reprinted by permission of Houghton Mifflin Company: 24, 26, 46, 56, 58, 64, 66, 72, 80, 82, 86, 88, 90, 94, 96, 102, 104, 110, 128, 136, 142, 144, 150, 152.

Rawlings, Marjorie Kinnan: excerpted from *The Yearling*. Copyright © 1938 by Marjorie Kinnan Rawlings. Copyright renewed © 1966 Norton Baskin. Reprinted by permission of Charles Scribner's Sons, an imprint of Macmillan Publishing Company: 30, 32.

Stevens, Wallace: from *The Collected Poems of Wallace Stevens*. Copyright © 1954 by Wallace Stevens. Reprinted by permission of Alfred A. Knopf, Inc.: 48, 50, 54, 62, 114, 146.

First frontispiece: A pair of bottlenose dolphins graces the open sea, Dolphin Research Center, Grassy Key

Second frontispiece: The evening heavens are illuminated over a tidal mangrove bay, Cape Romano–Ten Thousand Islands Aquatic Preserve, south of Marco

Third frontispiece: Tender new beech tree leaves announce the arrival of spring in an upland hardwood forest, Tallahassee

Title page: A laughing gull in its summer plumage rests on a tidal mud flat, Indian Key

Right: A hurricane leaves sponges and shells to adorn the Little Marco Pass Beach, Rookery Bay Aquatic Preserve, south of Naples

FOREWORD

Florida, the Sunshine State. Land of bright skies, perpetual warmth and sandy beaches. That's the quick-and-easy image that lures vast numbers of tourists and new residents to my native state.

Certainly the sun-and-beaches description is correct, as far as it goes. It says much, but leaves so much more unsaid about the natural beauties and intrigues of this southernmost part of the United States.

It's not just the promoters, visitors and newcomers whose perspective of Florida's natural magnitude is lacking. Most natives as well fail to appreciate just what we have and how tenuous its existence is in the face of burgeoning growth. Though born and reared in central Florida and a longtime outdoorsman, I shared those oversights until age 40.

In 1970, ambitious to be elected to the U.S. Senate and facing the realities of a going-nowhere campaign, I decided to walk from one end of the state to the other to prove that I was "down-to-earth" and willing to work harder than anyone else. From the red-clay farms and hardwood forests of northwestern Florida to the beckoning beaches and coral reefs of John Pennekamp State Park in the Keys, my trail stretched for well over a thousand miles.

It worked. I got the job . . . and an unexpected bonus that will long outlive the job. Step by step, I experienced Florida in its entirety, developing a vision of its varied riches and firming a commitment to their protection for generations to come. A sampling of my experiences:

One night I camped by a natural pool in the Blackwater Forest. The next morning, swimming "in the altogether" under a sumptuous sunrise, reinforced for me the importance of public access to such areas.

The Osceola National Forest exposed me to an array of trees, flowers, streams, swamps, birds and evidence of animal habitat. That memory later gave me the determination needed to push through legislation denying federal intent to allow strip mining for phosphate in the forest.

The Florida Sheriffs Boys Ranch sits on the banks of the famous Suwannee River. It gives dependent boys a magnificent natural surrounding where they can live and learn, and prepare for their future. My stopover provided one more example of the many ways an unfettered environment can serve human needs.

It was bright and 100 degrees the afternoon I left Gainesville and headed across Paynes Prairie. Suddenly, a thunderstorm took away the expansive, grassy view and refocused my attention on the path ahead. By the time I reached the far side of the prairie, I had tallied 42 dead snakes or snakeskins along the route, apparently victims of the elements.

"When you go down the beautiful Silver River from Silver Springs and into the Oklawaha, the idea that anything should change is certainly upsetting and I think we must be sure they are protected from damage." That diary entry from a boat tour, the only non-walking part of my journey, reflected growing concern about the potential effects of the Cross Florida Barge Canal construction. (I later initiated action that removed federal authority for the project.)

After a few days' trek past the picturesque beaches and seagulls of southwestern coastal communities from St. Petersburg to Ft. Myers, it was a dramatic change to turn due east and begin a 142-mile venture across the Everglades. For the most part I was alone, with an occasional alligator sunning, turtles, rabbits and vast numbers of birds — in the air, on the ground and in the trees. To the south was the favored territory of the scarce Florida panther. There was little to distract me from close examination of my surroundings, leaving ample time to contemplate the ecologic importance of this section of the state.

The result? In 1971 I proposed establishing the 574,000-acre Big Cypress National Preserve to help protect the fragile ecosystem serving Everglades National Park. Three years later it was established. A 146,000-acre addition to the preserve will expand watershed and wildlife habitat protection.

Heading south down the Atlantic coast from West Palm Beach — overgrown with people, cars and buildings — required another major environmental adjustment. But this, too, was Florida, offering splashes of magnificent scenery along the Gold Coast — waterfront, seafowl, glorious royal poinciana trees and skyscraping coconut palms.

On the 92nd day of walking I reached the end of my trail, John Pennekamp Coral Reef State Park with its white sands and undersea treasures lying offshore. This special place was later targeted by the U.S. Department of Interior's plan to lease nearby waters for oil and gas exploration, testimony that constant vigilance is necessary to thwart those who would destroy our precious heritage in the interest of commerce.

The education that I received on my trip imposed a lasting impression on my conscience and judgment. If all could have walked in my shoes, the task of protecting and preserving our environment would be no challenge at all.

Thus, this photographic essay, *Florida, Images of the Landscape*, has meaning beyond the breathtaking beauty portrayed by the work of James Valentine. The underlying message is that what we are seeing is real, irreplaceable and cannot be taken for granted.

— LAWTON CHILES

An ancient cypress witnesses the passage of day, Cypress Gardens, Winter Haven

Here are the faces of Florida. Here are the images of our environment diverse and beautiful. The perceptive skill of author/photographer James Valentine presents you with myriad vistas at once typical and unusual. This is the natural Florida without a single distracting man-made structure appearing in the book. You will see the true Florida at different times of the year, from unusual perspectives and caught in different lights from dawn to dusk.

Through Valentine's photographs you will travel from the beech and magnolia hardwood forests of the northern, temperate part of the state down to the tropical hardwood forests of the Florida Keys. As you head south, you will see the changing makeup of forests, swamps and marshes, and you will see enduring landscapes like the palm-crowded islands of the salt marshes.

Valentine has preserved the tender springtime of the northern woods and the great flare of summer flowers on the vast inland prairies. Always his technique is superb, and you will find yourself gazing intently and at length into the vistas he presents.

As the images in this collection emphasize, water is the major sculptor of Florida's landscapes. You will see the special and individual character of the famous Florida rivers: the mighty Apalachicola, the elegant Suwannee and the hauntingly beautiful Oklawaha. Florida's springs, those jewels of our waterways, are presented in all their exquisite color. Also set forth for your enjoyment are the great inland marshes such as Paynes Prairie, tree swamps where buttressed cypress and tupelo hold sway, and the incomparable Everglades — that river of grass 40 miles wide that flows from Lake Okeechobee to Florida Bay. The coastline images are particularly lovely and illustrate the variety of shoreline vistas found in Florida.

This book is for Floridians and visitors alike. It is for young people avid to know more about their natural environment, for their parents interested in seeing natural Florida firsthand, and for those who have seen this land for many, many years. The book will not only give you great pleasure as you read it, you will also find that Valentine's images will forever affect the way you view Florida. After reading *Florida, Images of the Landscape*, you will have a heightened awareness of the Florida that has engendered a powerful sense of loving stewardship in those who know her.

— MARJORIE H. CARR

Editor's Introduction

Their words span three centuries. They are writers and poets, biologists and botanists, artists and environmental activists. But the authors excerpted in this volume have one important trait in common: a deep and abiding love for the natural world.

Eighteenth-century botanist and ornithologist William Bartram was the first of this group to walk Florida's soil. He traversed the state while gathering material for his *Travels* in the 1780s, investigating, cataloguing and describing the plants and animals that he found. Fifty years later, artist and naturalist John James Audubon explored Florida, particularly the Keys. He recorded his findings in *Audubon's America* and *Audubon by Himself*. On his "Thousand-Mile Walk to the Gulf" in 1867, naturalist John Muir passed through Florida and documented his impressions in his journal, which was later published.

Poet Wallace Stevens, known for verse that contrasts reality with imagination, often turned to Florida seascapes for inspiration during the 1910s to 1930s. Marjorie Kinnan Rawlings memorialized northern Florida through her writings, most notably *The Yearling*, published in 1938. Field ecologist Archie Carr was a University of Florida zoology professor and the world's leading authority on sea turtles. He wrote nearly a dozen books and more than a hundred articles on natural history subjects. His wife, Marjorie, founded Florida Defenders of the Environment and remains one of the state's most politically active environmentalists.

Marjory Stoneman Douglas has been a Florida environmentalist and writer since the 1910s. She founded Friends of the Everglades and authored *The Everglades: River of Grass* and other volumes. Biologist and author Rachel Carson was also an active environmentalist, and is best known for her controversial *Silent Spring*, which spoke out against the dangers of chemical pesticides and herbicides.

More than 200 years have passed since William Bartram discovered the Alachua Sink, in what is now known as Paynes Prairie State Preserve. Yet his descriptions remain as sparkling as emerald light-filled waters or cypress on a crisp fall day — scenes discovered through James Valentine's camera lens. The timeless beauty of Florida's unspoiled landscapes — that is what binds together this collection of words and images.

— Margaret Terrell Morse

Gorgonia sea fans decorate the canyons of Looe Key Reef, Looe Key National Marine Sanctuary

JAMES VALENTINE

FLORIDA'S WILDERNESS WATERSPHERE
An Epic Photographic Journey Through Florida's Wilderness Heritage

The very nature of water celebrates the cyclical quality of life, as moisture not only forms drops in the atmosphere but continually flows in circles from sky to earth and earth to sky. The cycle of water's journey is more extensive in Florida than in any other part of the country, for it not only courses through porous limestone into the earth's great cavernous aquifers, but also surrounds the state in the ever-moving Atlantic Ocean and the Gulf of Mexico.

We are on a photographic quest with water as it circulates its essence into every aspect of wilderness life in the state of Florida. This wilderness watersphere journey is that story, depicting Florida's life-giving waters through environmental photographic art images.

The Wilderness Watersphere Journey

We have begun a timeless trek to witness a virgin land-scape of many facets. For millions of years the power of water has traveled through the Florida wilderness-scape, providing the foundation necessary for a semitropical landscape. Our wilderness watersphere journey follows this ancient water path tradition by depicting Florida's six major geographic life zones. In the course of our travels, we will witness pristine wilderness and wildlife habitats that the water provides with life.

Each spring, enormous thunderstorms form above the southeastern United States to release their largess upon the earth. This water filters through porous limestone, rocks, sand and clay to navigate along solution channels below the earth's surface. Out of aquifer cave systems below the surface of the earth, more than 300 major springs ascend into the semitropical environments of northern and central Florida. Many of these springs are first magnitude in size, flow and natural beauty. They are the sacred beginnings of creeks and streams which help create many of Florida's rivers and lakes. Along these lush waterways, we encounter hammocks, cypress ponds, swamps, piney flatwoods, scrub, live oak, palm glades and prairie communities.

The miracle of water life is celebrated as we make our way along the Atlantic and Gulf coasts. Here we witness the great estuaries of the coastal communities with their complex of hardwood hammocks, waterways, grassy mud flats, and salt marsh, sandbar and mangrove systems. Where seawater encounters the Florida coast, we explore wilderness beaches, savannahs and sand dune systems — that fragile white sand ribbon of life that surrounds much of the state.

Moving inland, we explore the enormous lake systems of central and southern Florida that act as reservoirs for the hauntingly beautiful Everglades. A foray into that famed wetland reveals a world of dramatic storms, great cypress swamps, grass prairies, sloughs, estuaries, mangroves, bay systems and the most extensive wilderness beaches in Florida.

The great waters of the Gulf and the Atlantic offer some of the most diverse sandbar and marine life in the world. We swim with the dolphins, see wilderness seascapes in the Keys, the Marquesas and the Dry Tortugas.

Environmental Art Photography

Air, light and water have wondrous, similar qualities. When these three elements enter an environmental space, they flow separately or together with the same permeating movement. This living movement in the photographic subject is the life-affirming element, an essential key to understanding the power behind each environmental image in this collection.

To more clearly understand the movement of air, light and water, it is necessary to quiet the mind, eliminating distracting thoughts to allow one's self to become a natural extension of the living landscape. Through this process of awareness, the photographer becomes so centered with his subject that he intuitively knows when to expose light to the film. In essence, mind and film mirror a beautiful universe. As the self becomes one with the subject, the resulting images, borrowed from the earth, celebrate the oneness of all life. The shutter clicks open at the peak of emotional and mental dialogue with the earth.

Animal Stories

Visiting Florida without appreciating its vast array of animal, insect, bird, fish and shellfish populations is to miss some of the most important living aspects of the state. Florida is a land where you can encounter very special animals and hear remarkable tales. In my extensive travels, I have had many dynamic animal experiences. Many are owed to unique organizations that are involved in professional wildlife rehabilitation and resident breeding research.

While photographing brown pelicans at the Suncoast Seabird Sanctuary, it became clear to me that each pelican had its own distinct personality. Some pelicans asked directly for food, others waited patiently, others ignored me, others tried to sneak the food, while some almost knocked over my camera to find it.

A bountiful natural bouquet of milkworts, hatpins, wiregrass and blazing stars decorates the National Audubon Kissimmee Prairie Preserve, north of Lake Okeechobee

The Suncoast Seabird Sanctuary's primary function is to serve as a hospital for the care and rehabilitation of injured and sick birds. Thousands of birds have been successfully treated and released from the sanctuary. Hundreds of birds arrive daily to visit their handicapped bird friends and to roost on top of the netted rehabilitation area.

Over the years, the sanctuary's reputation as a bird healing center has spread, not only among people, but also in the bird kingdom. On several occasions, sick and injured birds have shown up on their own, seemingly asking for help. On one such occasion, a brown pelican tangled up in fishing line accompanied by a sick pelican friend were waiting together after sunset at the sanctuary beach entrance. There is also a network of concerned citizens that calls the sanctuary when an injured bird is seen walking down the beach toward the hospital. "Pelican headed down the beach at 110th Street." "There's a pelican coming your way at 105th Street." And on down the line of beach condos.

While on location with a special permit to photograph the West Indian manatee at Homosassa Springs, I had a memorable experience. Images of the manatee were taken from inside a clear Plexiglas camera housing, open at the top, which allowed me access to all camera controls while seeing my subject through a special anti-distortion optical system at water level. There was enough room in my camera box to stow some carrots, a favorite snack of the manatee. Everything was going fine until one very ambitious manatee saw the carrots in my clear box. To my surprise, the gentle giant's nose was soon inches away, nudging and lifting my entire camera system out of the water. Yes! He immediately got a carrot!

It is a major event to wade into the center of the Fakahatchee Strand to locate "Guzmania Gulch," whimsically named by my guide, Ken Alvarez, an outstanding regional biologist for the Department of Natural Resources. After four hours of swamp challenges, we reached the cathedral palace of Guzmania. That's when things intensified. Two minutes after my photographing was completed, we heard what seemed to be a freight train approaching — a severe thunderstorm. It got very dark and rained so hard that visibility was reduced to 20 feet. Lightning cracked overhead only a few feet from where we were standing in waist-deep water.

I came out of the swamp that evening with greater respect for all life, including Florida's unofficial state bird, the mosquito. They don't get much credit for being a vital link in the estuarian and wetland food chain, feeding small fish which in turn feed the birds.

Speaking of bugs, . . . my father, Dr. J. Manson Valentine, a noted naturalist/scientist, once told me a classic Everglades insect story. "In 1932, we made an expedition at dusk in our Hudson Essex across the newly built Tamiami Trail across the Everglades. To our astonishment, we drove into an insect blizzard. We immediately placed a butterfly net out the window, gathering what turned out to be a quart jar of moths, beetles and bugs in a 10-mile section of the trail. That harvest yielded an estimated 144,000 specimens and brought several new insect species to science. This collecting trip coincided with the solar/lunar pull and the spring breeding season, which apparently stimulated the insects to swarm."

To the dolphin alone, beyond all others, nature has granted what the best philosophers seek: friendship for no advantage. Though it has no need at all of any man, yet it is a genial friend to all and has helped many. — Plutarch (46–120 A.D.)

Dolphins are simply amazing mammals. Through the eons their presence has been one of peace with the environment and has been honored by human cultures throughout the world. They have evolved on a parallel path with man, developing a brain of similar intelligence, but with certain special attributes. Dolphin consciousness is comprised of the spontaneous joy of living and the wisdom to share their form of freedom with others. My encounters with the dolphins at the Dolphin Research Center during open water exercises were filled with awe and delight. Dolphins who work closely with human desires respond favorably to commands only if they come from the heart. In fact, when given a joyful command, they do their own creative variation of the request, thus avoiding boredom. The performance goes beyond expectations as if they are saying, "We are here to teach you the meaning of spontaneous, compassionate freedom."

Diviner than the dolphin is nothing yet created: for indeed they were aforetime men . . . . — Oppian (Halieutica)

As Floridians move into the 21st century and wilderness areas come under developmental pressure, we all have the opportunity and privilege to honor in our hearts and with our actions the great diversity of life found in this state. Habitat protection of entire environmental systems is critical, first and foremost. The resident breeding programs associated with brown pelicans, dolphins, panthers and West Indian manatees are tremendous success stories. Through professional research, dedicated people have offered regeneration for many species as a potential back-up system in parallel evolution with protection of the species in their native habitats.

— JAMES VALENTINE

This book is dedicated to my father, whom I honor as a co-naturalist, and to the dolphins who have taught me the real meaning of freedom.

Emerald light-filled waters gush from the ancient Ladies Parlor Spring, Silver Springs

NORTHERN FLORIDA

You are on an ancient journey through the wilderness watersphere, as old as the primeval forest. Beneath the great hardwood forests of Florida's north country, aquifers release bubbling spring water that permeates the landscape. Join these crystalline waters as they gush from springs into cypress ponds opening onto meandering streams. Enter a world of river valleys and lakes bounded by hardwood forests. Witness immense bluffs and rolling hills overlooking forested floodplains. Explore enormous fern-clad sink holes and cave formations. Traverse vast prairies dotted with marigolds and lazy alligators.

Northern Florida's landscape is the beginning of a subtropical paradise, rich in bird life and home to many rare and endangered animals. You have begun your quest, experiencing Florida much the way it was before the advent of modern man.

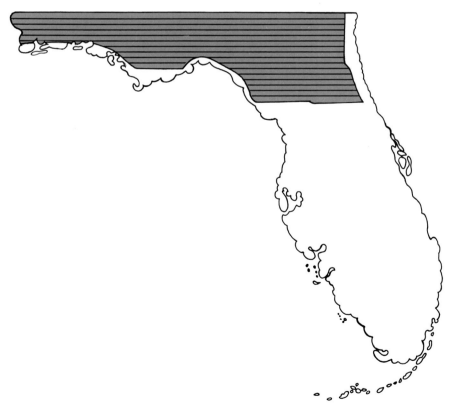

*Left: Red maple leaves sprinkle the earth with fall color,
Lake Iamonia, Tallahassee*

Above: A Florida bobcat kitten plays on a pine limb, St. John's County

An unusually dry season leaves mammoth cypress buttresses
exposed to the winter winds, Apalachicola National Forest

An upland hardwood forest yields to a remote spring filled
with spatterdock, an aquatic plant, Jackson County

Overleaf: Fog wisps dance upon the swirling waters of
Cypress Springs, Washington County

"The Cuppressus disticha [cypress] stands in the first order of North
American trees. Its majestic stature is surprising; and on approaching it,
we are struck with a kind of awe, at beholding the stateliness of the trunk,
lifting its cumbrous top towards the skies, and casting a wide shade upon
the ground, as a dark intervening cloud, which, for a time, excludes the
rays of the sun." — William Bartram

Winter explosion of color over north Florida, Tallahassee

Cypress trees drink in the mist at Blue Hole, part of the
headwaters of Ichetucknee Springs,
Ichetucknee Springs State Park, Fort White

"How glorious the powerful sun, minister of the Most
High in the rule and government of this earth, leaves our
hemisphere, retiring from our sight beyond the western
forests! I behold with gratitude his departing smiles, tinging
the fleecy roseate clouds, now riding far away on the
eastern horizon; behold they vanish from sight in the azure
skies!" — William Bartram

Crystal River limestone formations decorate the Cathedral Room,
Florida Caverns State Park, Marianna

Flame azalea bursts forth along the high bluffs of the
Apalachicola River, Torreya State Park, Bristol

"*P*lants *are credited with but dim and uncertain
sensation, and minerals with positively none at all. But why
may not even a mineral arrangement of matter be endowed
with sensation of a kind that we in our blind exclusive
perfection can have no manner of communication with?*"
— *John Muir*

---

*Alum Bluff is the highest bluff in Florida and faces west toward a
magnificent floodplain forest, The Nature Conservancy's
Apalachicola Bluffs and Ravines Preserve*

*Golden light weaves through swamp azalea at the Garden of Eden,
the historical name for The Nature Conservancy's preserve,
Liberty County*

*Overleaf: Cypress trees on a crisp fall day in Pine Log Swamp,
Washington County*

---

*"October 18 [1867]. . . . It is said that not a point in all Florida is
more than three hundred feet above sea-level — a country where
but little grading is required for roads, but much bridging, and
boring of many tunnels through forests." — John Muir*

By midsummer, the once-raging spring torrents of the
Alapaha River go underground and only segments of this stream
flow gently across sandbars, Hamilton County

Peacock Springs is a world-renowned scuba diving site
which opens into a vast subterranean network of caves,
Suwannee County

"The sinkhole was a phenomenon common to the
Florida limestone regions. Underground rivers ran
through such sections. . . .

A giant live oak hides in an unknown world accessible during
the annual Suwannee River spring flood, Hamilton County

A mammoth shaft of hollowed-out limestone forms one of
Florida's most dynamic sinkholes,
Falling Waters State Recreation Area, Chipley

. . . The bubbling springs that turned at once into creeks
and runs were outbreaks of these. Sometimes a thin shell of
surface soil caved in and a great cavern was revealed, with
or without a flow of water." — Marjorie Kinnan Rawlings

---

*Alligators bask among marsh marigolds at the Alachua Sink,
Paynes Prairie State Preserve, Gainesville*

*Spleenwort, cinnamon and maidenhair fern decorate a rockland
hammock sinkhole at Paynes Prairie State Preserve, Gainesville*

*Overleaf: Spring brings new life to an upland hardwood forest of
dogwood, white oak and beech trees, Torreya State Park, Bristol*

"*In and about the Great Sink, are to be seen incredible
numbers of crocodiles, some of which are of an enormous
size, and view the passenger with incredible impudence and
avidity.*" — *William Bartram*

The panther, Florida's most endangered mammal, can be seen
in its ancestral surroundings, a unique environmental habitat at
the Tallahassee Junior Museum, Tallahassee

The Wakulla Spring Run displays a year-round bounty of
wildlife including white ibis and limpkin,
Edward Ball Wakulla Springs State Park, Wakulla Springs

"Most of us walk unseeing through the world, unaware
alike of its beauties, its wonders, and the strange and
sometimes terrible intensity of the lives that are being lived
about us." — Rachel Carson

Water elms preside along the Apalachicola River floodplain forest,
the bluffs below Lake Seminole

By late fall, the Suwannee River exposes its rocky canyon
bottom at Big Shoals State Park, north of White Springs

"... we begin to feel something of that relentlessly pressing
force by which nature controls her own." — Rachel Carson

The meandering Suwannee joins a spring run coming out of
Suwannee River State Park, Live Oak

Cinnamon ferns and violets create an enchanted scene,
Devil's Millhopper State Geological Site, Gainesville

"This enchanting little forest is partly encircled by a deep
creek, a branch of the river, that has its source in the high
forests . . . and winds through the extensive grassy plains
which surround this peninsula, to an almost infinite
distance, and then unites its waters with
those of the river. . . ." — William Bartram

GULF
COAST

Barrier islands are magical places where light, water and form interplay to celebrate the love of creation. This string of islands and wetland plant communities stretches south from Perdido Key to the Ten Thousand Islands, protecting the coast from erosion and providing a habitat for wildlife.

The Gulf Coast offers a great diversity of landscape forms: along the Panhandle coastline, expansive white sand beaches join emerald-colored seas; the wild Big Bend wilderness area encompasses more than 150 miles of salt marshes bound by hardwood hammocks; to the south, West Indian manatees navigate through some of the largest mangrove swamps in the world. To see the gulf marshes from the air is to witness a remarkable energy-absorbing system whose heart is the pumping action of the tides.

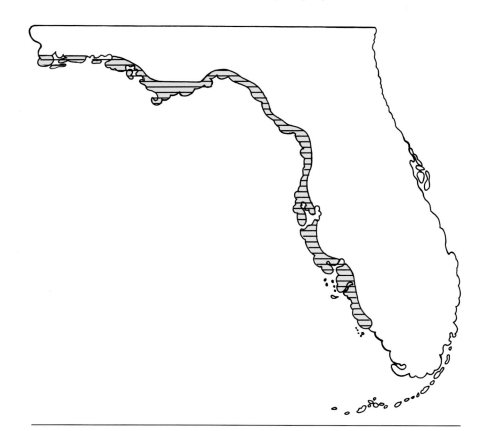

Left: Evening summer storms drop golden light-filled rain on the Gulf of Mexico, Cayo Costa State Park, Boca Grande

Above: Florida white pelicans mainly inhabit the wild estuarian bays of the Gulf Coast; here they groom in unison at the Cypress Gardens wading bird exhibit for injured birds, Winter Haven

Alligator Lake, a coastal dune lake, hosts a community
of cattails and water lilies, St. Andrews State Recreation Area,
Panama City

Shell forms catch shifting beach sands,
St. Joseph Peninsula State Park, Port St. Joe

"*All the winds were hushed and the calm of the
heavens was as profound as that of the palmy islands
and their encircling waters . . . enclosed by the
sunset-colored dome. . . .*" — John Muir

Moonlit sabal palms are mirrored into the blackwater
Waccasassa River, Waccasassa Bay State Preserve

Exposed manatee grass glows on tidal mud flats, which play
an important role in the estuarian food chain,
Cape Romano–Ten Thousand Islands Aquatic Preserve,
south of Marco

"As the immense dew of Florida
Brings forth
The big-finned palm
And green vine angering for life, . . .

Bowing to a warm, early fall breeze, sea oats proclaim a
harvest moon, St. George Island State Park, Eastpoint

A fall celebration of hair grasses, saw palmetto and broomsedge
brightens the savannah on Caladesi Island,
Caladesi Island State Park, Dunedin

Overleaf: Severe summer lightning storms frequent many of
the barrier islands, Cayo Costa State Park, Boca Grande

. . . As the immense dew of Florida
    Brings forth hymn and hymn
    From the beholder,
    . . . .
    So, in me, come flinging
    Forms, flames, and the flakes of flames." — Wallace Stevens

Florida white pelicans soar over their winter estuarian feeding and roosting grounds, Chassahowitzka National Wildlife Refuge, Homosassa

First light paints a sable palm on the beach goldenrod-covered dunes of St. Joseph Peninsula State Park, Port St. Joe

"Barque of phosphor
on the palmy beach,

Move outward into heaven,
Into the alabasters
And night blues. . . ." — Wallace Stevens

Late evening glow envelops the vast reaches of Tampa Bay,
Tampa/St. Petersburg

Primeval hydric hammocks adjacent to vast marsh systems,
Big Bend Coast

"*One day in January I climbed to the housetop to get
a view of another of the fine sunsets of this land of flowers.
The landscape was a strip of clear Gulf water, a strip of
sylvan coast, a tranquil company of shell and coral keys,
and a gloriously colored sky without a threatening cloud.*"
— John Muir

Sun penetrates a sand dollar the size of a baby's fingernail,
Sanibel Island

Delicacies of light cast their magic through hairgrass,
Caladesi Island State Park, Dunedin

Overleaf: A fecund black needle rush habitat provides a nursery
for many sea creatures, St. Mark's National Wildlife Refuge,
St. Mark's

"Not a pine, not a palm, in all this garden excels these stately grass
plants in beauty of wind-waving gestures. Here are panicles that are one
mass of refined purple; others that have flowers as yellow as ripe oranges,
and stems polished and shining like steel wire. . . . But all of them are
beautiful beyond the reach of language." — John Muir

Edge of day brings life to a pristine maritime forest — a coastal dune lake and scrub community of rosemary, scrub oak, slash pine and sand pine, Topsail Hill, east of Destin

First dawn glow paints another day over the beaches of St. George Island, St. George Island State Park, Eastpoint

"*Foam and cloud are one.*
Sultry moon-monsters
Are dissolving.
. . . .
There will never be an end
To this droning of the surf." — *Wallace Stevens*

During lean winter months, brown pelicans ensure their own
survival by feeding at the Suncoast Seabird Sanctuary,
Indian Shores

Roseate spoonbills bask in ebbing light at their traditional
mud flat feeding grounds, J.N. "Ding" Darling National
Wildlife Refuge, Sanibel

"*There is an extensive shallow on the coast, close by,*
which the receding tide exposes daily. . . .

Brown pelicans take shelter from frigid winter winds on Rookery Island, Rookery Bay Aquatic Preserve, Rookery Bay National Estuarine Research Reserve, south of Naples

Changing tides expose sand flats south of Little Marco Pass Beach, Rookery Bay Aquatic Preserve, south of Naples

Overleaf: Perdido Beach glows with the beginning of a new day, Perdido Key State Recreation Area, Pensacola

. . . This is the feeding-ground of thousands of waders of all sizes, plumage, and language, and they make a lively picture and noise when they gather. . . ." — John Muir

*Meandering tidal creeks create an aerial estuarine mosaic,
Big Bend Coast*

*Red maple, sabal palm, saw grass and red cedar mingle on a
hydric hammock along Halls River, Homosassa Springs*

"*Behold yon promontory, projecting far into the great
river, beyond the still lagoon, half a mile distant from me:
what a magnificent grove arises on its banks! how glorious
the Palm!*" — William Bartram

Known as Walking Trees by the Seminoles, red mangrove trees
share a swamp with black mangroves and oyster beds, part of
Florida's estimated 469,000 acres of mangrove forests,
Cape Romano–Ten Thousand Islands Aquatic Preserve,
south of Marco

Heavy winds create sea streaks of churned-up water,
Big Bend Coast

"*The* land is still encroaching on the sea, and it does
so not evenly, in a regular line, but in fringing lagoons and
inlets and dotlike coral islands." — John Muir

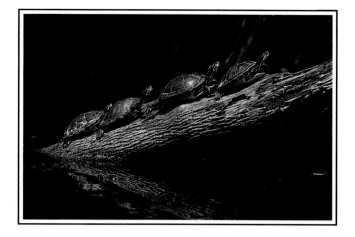

CENTRAL FLORIDA

Sabal palms, common to the heart of Florida, are found in a land influenced by spring- and rain-fed lakes. Pine flatwoods inhabit vast stretches of central Florida and are the predominant vegetation community. To evoke the distant past, stand on a three- to seven-million-year-old shoreline and watch the sun penetrate fog over a rare scrub community. Traverse prairie grasslands whose mesic oak and palm hammocks stretch for miles.

The springs found in this part of Florida contribute greatly to the eight billion gallons of water that are delivered daily by the state's 300 major springs. Central Florida is a merging point of subtropical and tropical communities that rivals the rain forest in magnitude and food production.

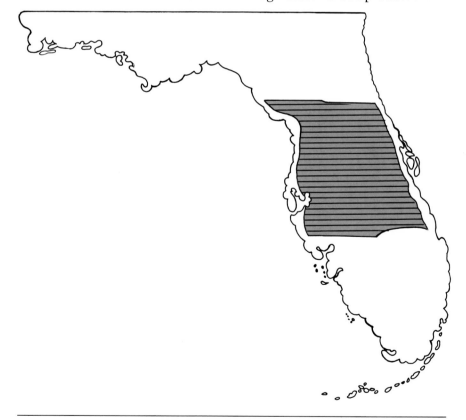

Left: Florida's state tree, the distinguished sabal palm, awaits passage into another day, upper Myakka Lake, Myakka River State Park, Sarasota

Above: Red-bellied turtles sun themselves on the banks of Silver River, Silver Springs

Overleaf: Dawn penetrates a rosemary scrub bald, an intricate ecosystem that supports rosemary, sand pine and scrub oaks, Highlands County

Our national symbol, the endangered bald eagle, makes its home in the wilds of Florida and is protected by Save Our American Raptors (S.O.A.R.), Apopka

A primeval cypress giant stands as a reminder of the pristine swamp forests that once covered most of Florida, Wekiwa Springs watershed, Apopka

"*Lowlands, wherever they occurred, were covered with cypress draped with Spanish beard moss and dense bushes of the magnolia family, growing in black mud.*"
— *John James Audubon*

Tannic acid, a natural leaching product found in decaying leaves,
colors the Florida waters with a beautiful but harmless
reddish stain, Seminole County

Crystal-clear spring waters ripple from the base of a sabal palm,
palmetto and spleenwort, Seminole County

"*October 20 [1867]. Swamp very dense during this
day's journey. Almost one continuous sheet of water
covered with aquatic trees and vines. No stream that I
crossed to-day appeared to have the least idea where it was
going.*" — John Muir

In an ancient ritual, fog ascends from the Blue Spring Run and
provides a canopy for live oaks and a habitat for West Indian
manatee, Blue Spring State Park, Orange City

Caretaker of the forest, a barred owl looks for fish along the
Blue Spring Run, Blue Spring State Park, Orange City

Overleaf: A summer storm sustains the mesic flatwoods and
palmetto prairie, Archbold Biological Station, Highlands County

"*The streams of Florida are still young, and in many
places are untraceable. . . . Florida streams are not yet
possessed of banks and braes and definite channels. . . .*

Late summer rains flood hardwood hammocks bordering
Myakka River State Park, Sarasota

Acres of lotus and pickerelweed reach toward the hot noonday sun,
Lake Kissimmee State Park, Lake Wales

*. . . Their waters in deep places are black as ink, perfectly
opaque, and glossy on the surface as if varnished. It is often
difficult to ascertain which way they are flowing or
creeping, so slowly and so widely do they circulate through
the tree-tangles and swamps of the woods. . . .*

*Stillness and light are the preservation of wildness,
Lower Wekiva River State Reserve, Sanford*

*The Oklawaha River flows wild and free as a living symbol of our
precious environmental heritage, Marion County*

*. . . Most streams appear to travel through a country with
thoughts and plans for something beyond. But those of
Florida are at home, do not appear to be traveling at all,
and seem to know nothing of the sea."* — *John Muir*

*Limpkin neatly arranged these apple snail shells after a gourmet
feast, Silver River State Park, Silver Springs*

*The eerie calls of the limpkin can be heard along Silver River
State Park, Silver Springs*

*Overleaf: At the headwaters of the Rainbow River is one of
Florida's clearest springs, which is protected and designated
by the state as an aquatic preserve, Dunnellon*

"Why should man value himself as more than a small part of
the one great unit of creation? . . . The universe would be
incomplete without man; but it would also be incomplete without
the smallest transmicroscopic creature that dwells beyond our
conceitful eyes and knowledge." — John Muir

Golden morning light embraces the thousand-pound limbs of a live oak seeking perfect balance, Lake Kissimmee State Park, Lake Wales

A mammoth live oak presides at the entrance to Lake Griffin State Recreation Area, Fruitland Park

"[*The* live oak] is a grand old king, whose crown gleamed in the bright sky long ere the Spanish shipbuilders felled a single tree of this noble species." — *John Muir*

*Turkey oaks and young longleaf pines stand like bristly elves
in a sandhill community, Lower Wekiva River State Preserve,
Sanford*

*Fern Hammock Springs, a crystalline spring grotto, nestles
among hardwood hammocks, Ocala National Forest*

*"I am now in the hot gardens of the sun, where the palm
meets the pine . . . strange plants, strange winds blowing
gently, whispering, cooing, in a language I never learned,
and strange birds also, everything solid or spiritual full of
influences that I never before felt. . . ." — John Muir*

One of the few places in Florida where humans can encounter
the docile West Indian manatee at close range, Homosassa Springs

A cormorant positions itself on a piece of driftwood overlooking
the Rainbow River, Dunnellon

"*But all the reason anybody really needs for saving
manatees is that they are fabulously outlandish and lovable
beasts . . . distantly related to elephants [and] strongly
modified for aquatic life.'* — Archie Carr

ATLANTIC COAST

The mighty Atlantic can display an air of extreme calm or it can exude a magnitude of force that creates new island sandbars virtually overnight and removes entire maritime forests. The Atlantic coast inherited the longest beaches in the state — extending from Amelia Island to Miami Beach. A few miles inland and north of Melbourne Beach, you can begin a trip on the headwaters of the St. John's River. At its mouth you can follow deep canyons of marsh grass-covered mud banks, filled with organic matter rich in nutrients and calories. The marsh is like the movement of a wild herd of animals, with billions of organisms working in unison to forge a single unit, linked by water, driven by the wind and harnessed to the sun to sustain life.

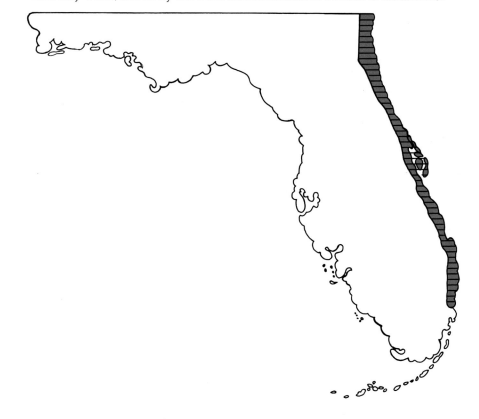

Left: Golden fire rises over the Atlantic, Little Talbot Island State Park, Fort George

Above: The prehistoric American crocodile has evolved for more than 160 million years with little change and today is highly endangered, Alligator Farm environmental habitat, St. Augustine

The floodplain marshes of the upper St. John's River provide
sustenance for isolated hammocks, cypress trees, smartweed
and senecio, Tosohatchee State Reserve, Christmas

Morning light uncovers a hidden terrain of coquina limestone,
a coastal rockbarren habitat, Washington Oaks State Gardens,
St. Augustine

"October 15 [1867]. To-day, at last, I reached Florida, the
so-called 'Land of Flowers,' that I had so long waited for, . . .
here it is, at the distance of a few yards! — a flat, watery, reedy
coast, with clumps of mangrove and forests of moss-dressed,
strange trees appearing low in the distance." — John Muir

Primordial duckweed swirls around an American alligator,
Alligator Farm environmental habitat, St. Augustine

Natural erosion exposes intertidal rock formations on the
south end of Big Talbot Island, Big Talbot Island State Park,
Fort George

"*This star, our own good earth, made many a successful
journey around the heavens ere man was made, and whole
kingdoms of creatures enjoyed existence and returned to
dust ere man appeared to claim them. After human beings
have also played their part in Creation's plan, they too may
disappear without any general burning or extraordinary
commotion whatever.*" — John Muir

The largest Anastasia limestone outcrop on the Atlantic coast,
Blowing Rocks Preserve, The Nature Conservancy, Tequesta

The Canaveral National Seashore coastline forms a protective
barrier for the Merrit Island National Wildlife Refuge, Titusville

Overleaf: Sandy mud flats document the movement of tide and
wind, Little Talbot Island State Park, Fort George

"*But yet, how awfully great and sublime is the majestic scene eastward!
the solemn sound of the beating surf strikes our ears; the dashing of yon
liquid mountains, like mighty giants, in vain assail the skies; they are
beaten back, and fall prostrate upon the shores of the trembling island.*"
— William Bartram

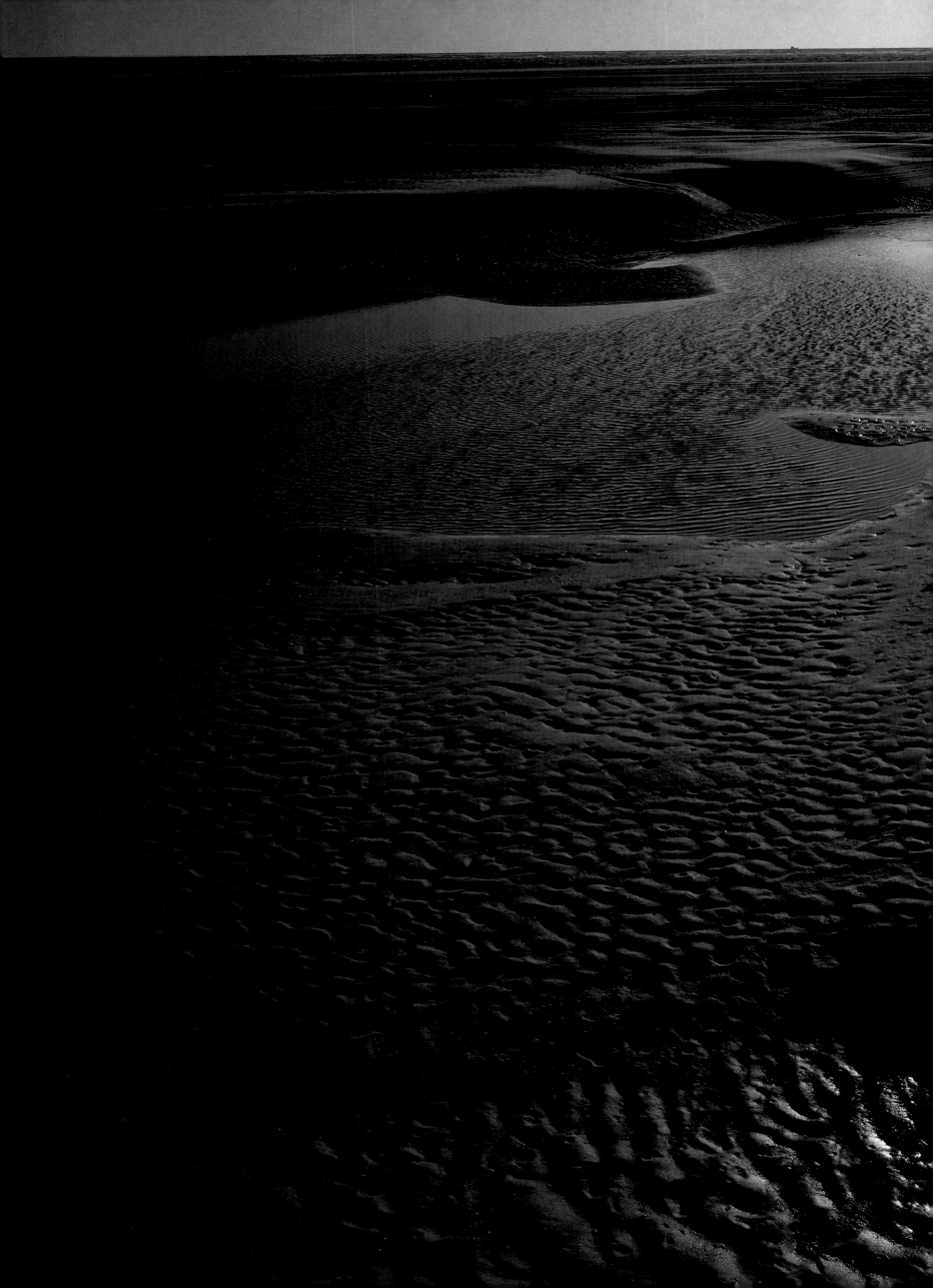

This Nature Conservancy maritime tidal marsh preserve provides
a buffer zone that protects the mainland from hurricanes and
provides a nursery for sea creatures, The Honorable Theodore
Roosevelt Preserve, Jacksonville

Nature's eternal cycle: the power of the sea and the sand whirl
into the red cedar; the power of the rain-soaked cedar dissolves
into the sea, south end of Big Talbot Island,
Big Talbot Island State Park, Fort George

"They tell us that plants are perishable, soulless
creatures, that only man is immortal, etc.; but this, I think,
is something that we know very nearly nothing about."
— John Muir

The Guana River marsh is one of the richest, most productive
systems on earth and provides continuous food for wildlife,
Guana River State Park, north of St. Augustine

Upper St. John's River floodplain marshes from the air during
extreme high water conditions, Tosohatchee State Reserve,
Christmas

" . . . if you want to visualize the anatomy of a region in a
short while the best possible means of travel is by a plane
flown sympathetically, searchingly and at an elevation
from which one kind of vegetation can be told from
another." — Archie Carr

Late evening wisps of sunset colors grace the shores of
John D. MacArthur Beach State Park, North Palm Beach

Shifting tides and currents create heavy seas at
Rattlesnake Island Inlet, north of Marineland

Overleaf: A soft full moon lends tranquility to a sabal palm
hammock, Merritt Island National Wildlife Refuge, Titusville

"The sea-clouds whitened far below the calm
And moved, as blooms move, in the swimming green
And in its watery radiance, while the hue

Of heaven in an antique reflection rolled
Round those flotillas. And sometimes the sea
Poured brilliant iris on the glistening blue." — Wallace Stevens

SOUTHERN FLORIDA

The golden flower-covered prairies of Lake Okeechobee create the upper boundary of southern Florida. Wet and dry prairie communities, with their luxuriant spread of grasses and bushes, truly manifest heaven on earth. Lake Okeechobee, the largest body of fresh water outside of the Great Lakes, is like a vast ocean of energy where storms can whip up gigantic waves in hours.

Water from Okeechobee regulates the abundance of life for southern Florida. It flows south to form the Everglades — a 40-mile-wide river only inches deep that creeps seaward on a slope of inches per mile. *Pa-hay-okee*, meaning "grassy water," is the Seminole name for these freshwater marshes, which are unique in all the world and cover most of the Everglades.

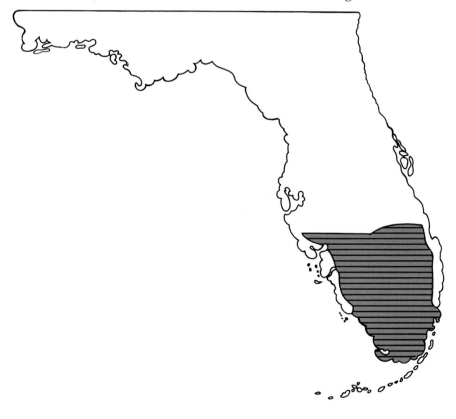

Left: Radiant yellow milkworts dominate the wetland prairie community of the National Audubon's Kissimmee Prairie Preserve, north of Lake Okeechobee

Above: A rare glimpse of a wild flamingo taking to the air, Everglades National Park

*Skies catch on fire over a tidal mud flat dotted with
white and brown pelicans, Everglades National Park, Flamingo*

*A tiny green tree frog rests on the roots of a strangler fig,
Fakahatchee Strand State Preserve, Copeland*

*"Frogs do for the night what birds do for the day: they
give it a voice. . . . because they sing mainly at night when
most birds are quiet they give the wet places much of their
incomparable nighttime atmosphere."*
— *Archie Carr*

Hair grasses become moving art forms in the natural glades of
Chekika State Recreation Area, Homestead

A potpourri of scallop pecten shells protrudes from tidal mud flats,
Everglades National Park

Overleaf: By mid-June the royal poinciana is in full blossom,
decorating most of the Miami-area landscape, Coral Gables

"The sponges, the corals, the shellfish, some of the crabs
along these coasts, the tiniest shell forms that turn up in the
muck below the oldest saw grass, are older than the whole
shape of this land." — Marjory Stoneman Douglas

Swamp lilies adorn marl prairie cypress savannahs,
Big Cypress National Preserve

Early morning dew glistens on the branches of a dwarf cypress,
Everglades National Park

"In the first sunlight the dew, a miracle of freshness,
stands on every leaf and wall and petal, in the finest of tiny
patterns, in bold patterns of wide-strung cobwebs; like
pearls in a silvery melting frostwork. The slant yellow sun
of winter dries it up in the next hour but all the secret roots
are nourished by it in the dry ground."
— Marjory Stoneman Douglas

A golden shower tree dips its branches into the blue heavens,
Coconut Grove

High noon clouds reflect a patchwork of colors over the wildest
beaches in Florida, looking north between East Cape and
Middle Cape, Everglades National Park

"
. . . a close forest of trees, every one in flower, and bent
down and entangled to network by luxuriant, bright-
blooming vines, and over all a flood of bright sunlight."
— John Muir

A concentration of water lettuce is a unique biological feature at
the National Audubon's Corkscrew Swamp Sanctuary, Naples

This labyrinthian maze of mangrove islands is part of the
remarkable Ten Thousand Islands, Everglades National Park

Overleaf: Hidden in the depths of the Fakahatchee Strand is a
pondapple slough alive with bromeliads and orchids,
Fakahatchee Strand State Preserve, Copeland

" . . . the rivers move silent and enormous from the saw
grass to the mangrove, and so to the sea, linked by
innumerable streams and cuts and channels, utterly
bewildering, never completely known."
— Marjory Stoneman Douglas

---

*A great blue heron stalks small fish near the Anhinga Trail,
Everglades National Park*

*Marsh grasses move in concert with the clouds and wind,
Observation Shoal, Lake Okeechobee*

"*The thin trill of a cone-headed cricket came from
somewhere in the grass, and along the shore a squawking
great blue heron flew off into the darkness. . . . Then a
lightning flash printed a spread-winged image of the heron
against the sky. . . .*" — *Archie Carr*

A rare stand of Florida royal palms protrudes above the
forest canopy, Fakahatchee Strand State Preserve, Copeland

*A dramatic winter storm at sunrise moves across the east shore
of Lake Okeechobee, Okeechobee*

"*What a landscape! Only palms as far as the eye
could reach! Smooth pillars rising from the grass, each
capped with a sphere of leaves, shining in the sun as bright
as a star. The silence and calm were as deep as ever I
found. . . .*" — John Muir

THE KEYS

Mirrored landscapes in motion dance upon the waters to reflect in us that our quest is almost complete. The Florida Keys are ancient reef systems continually rebuilding and decaying under the life-sustaining action of the oceans, weather and sun. Nowhere on this continent can you find such radiant tropical waters so verdant with intricate varieties of marine life.

North America's largest coral reef system begins outside Key Biscayne and continues south to Boca Grande Key south of Key West. The Keys provide a refuge for the key deer and a niche for several spectacular species of cactus. Thousands of aquatic birds weave through a Caribbean atmosphere to find a home among the mangrove islands on the gulf side of the Keys. Symbols of freedom pervade the Keys: follow a little loggerhead turtle as it forges ahead with all-knowing faith into the sea or rekindle your spirit with the dolphins, who are joyous friends to all.

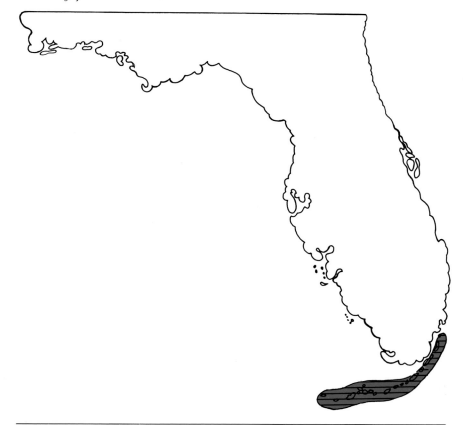

Left: A distant sandbar seems to float over the glassy waters of the Dry Tortugas, Fort Jefferson National Monument

Above: The rookery on Bush Key is a favorite nesting site of the brown noddy tern, Fort Jefferson National Monument

Overleaf: Mosquito Bank Reef exudes an abundance of brain coral and gorgonia sea fans, John Pennekamp Coral Reef State Park, Key Largo

Slow gradations of depth are seen in beautiful channels carved
by ocean currents and weather changes,
National Key Deer Refuge

Summer storms with five- to eight-mile-high thunderheads
bring much-needed fresh water to the Keys, Key West

"*I could see no striving in those magnificent wave-motions,
no raging; all the storm was apparently inspired with
nature's beauty and harmony. Every wave was obedient
and harmonious as the smoothest ripple of a forest lake,
and after dark all the water was phosphorescent like silver
fire, a glorious sight.*" — John Muir

Sun rays dance at dawn in the clouds and coconut palm fronds
on the east shore of Elliott Key, Biscayne National Park

A Caribbean atmosphere pervades the Elliott Key shoreline,
Biscayne National Park

"*The palms had full possession and appeared to
enjoy their sunny home. There was no jostling, no apparent
effort to outgrow each other. Abundance of sunlight was
there for every crown, and plenty to fall between. I walked
enchanted in their midst.*" — John Muir

Fish dance in the sun rays of the Dry Tortugas,
Fort Jefferson National Monument

Tempered light skims across the wild vastness of the
Marquesas Keys, Key West National Wildlife Refuge

Overleaf: Time stands motionless as the calm Atlantic moves
giant clouds with a delicate breath, near Conch Key

"*The sovereign clouds came clustering. The conch
Of loyal conjuration trumped. The wind
Of green blooms turning crisped the motley hue*

*To clearing opalescence. Then the sea
And heaven rolled as one and from the two
Came fresh transfigurings of freshest blue.*" — Wallace Stevens

The endangered key deer is the smallest deer in North America
and takes refuge on Big Pine Key, National Key Deer Refuge

Gumbo limbo ("naked Indian") trees inhabit the rockland
hammock community of Big Pine Key, National Key Deer Refuge

"*I have precious little sympathy for the selfish
propriety of civilized man, and if a war of races should
occur between the wild beasts and Lord Man I would be
tempted to sympathize with the bears.*" — John Muir

Spiral-gilled tube worms, measuring one-half inch high, cling to
the surface of porous coral, Looe Key National Marine Sanctuary

A butterfly orchid paints an intimate scene with two
miniature bromeliads, National Key Deer Refuge

"How strangely we are blinded to beauty and color,
form and motion, by comparative size! . . . Compared with
other things in God's creation the difference is nothing. We
all are only microscopic animalcula." — John Muir

A newborn loggerhead turtle, following an ancient instinctive
ritual, scurries past a horse conch shell on its way to the sea,
Bahia Honda State Recreation Area, Bahia Honda Key

A very rare semaphore cactus grows in a cactus barren,
lower Keys

Overleaf: A school of blue tangs moves briskly through the
semi-tropical waters of Key Largo Dry Rocks reef,
Key Largo National Marine Sanctuary, Key Largo

"Along with all other kinds of sea turtles, the loggerhead is
declining the world over. Its reproduction is increasingly hindered
by the loss of wild seashore and by the egg hunting that still goes
on in parts of the nesting range." — Archie Carr

ACKNOWLEDGEMENTS

This compendium of images represents the most diverse collection of photographic wilderness art ever assembled in one book depicting the natural beauty of Florida. Many years went into the research and development of these images, including a broad variety of transportation methods and technical support systems. The dedication of the people involved was supportive in every way, and their logistical help and equipment utilized were invaluable.

With great respect and special thanks, I wish to acknowledge the following organizations that helped make this book possible: The Alligator Farm; Archbold Biological Station; The Conservation Foundation Environmental Information Center, Winter Park, Florida; Cypress Gardens; Dolphin Research Center; Florida Audubon Society, Maitland, Florida; Florida Defenders of the Environment, Gainesville, Florida; Florida Department of Natural Resources; Florida Game and Fresh Water Fish Commission; Florida Manatee Research Educational Foundation; Florida Natural Areas Inventory; Florida Water Management Districts; Florida Wildlife Federation, Tallahassee, Florida; Homosassa Springs; E. Leitz Inc.; Marine Science Center; Morningside Nature Center, Gainesville, Florida; National Audubon Society; National Oceanic and Atmospheric Administration; National Park Service; The Nature Conservancy, Winter Park, Florida; Nikon Professional Services; Quest Foundation — Conservation Educational Center for the Advancement of Environmental Art Photography; The Rare Feline Breeding Center, Inc.; Save-A-Turtle; Save Our American Raptors (S.O.A.R.); Sierra Club, San Francisco, California; Silver Springs; Suncoast Seabird Sanctuary; Tallahassee Junior Museum; United Star Animals (U.S.A.); U.S. Fish and Wildlife Service.

Special recognition needs to be given to a number of people: Robert E. Baudy (Rare Feline Cat Breeder); Jim Cox (Ornithologist); Mr. & Mrs. Walter Driggers (Rainbow River Aquatic Preserve); The Staff at the Florida Natural Areas Inventory: Dennis Hardin (Research Ecologist), Dale Jackson (Research Zoologist) and Jim Muller (Coordinator); Ervin & Beth Jackson (Support); Roger L. Hammer (Naturalist); Ralph Heath (Bird Rehabilitator); Doris Mager (Raptor Education & Protection); Sid & Sue McCarty (Expedition Support); Chuck Olson (Conservationist); Pat Purcell (Environmental Science); Mandy & Jane Rodriguez (Dolphin Research); David Russell (Photographic exhibits, Russell Image Processing, Atlanta); Vi Rusk (Support); Captain Ed Toth (Wildlife Photographer & Nature Guide); Dr. Jesse R. White (Manatee Research & Protection); Anne Williams (Naturalist); Larry Wilson (Master Color Processor, Meteor, Atlanta).

I am grateful to Steve Gatewood, one of Florida's finest naturalists, for the hours spent on environmental research and text editing. In gratitude for support from Silver Springs, made possible by Mr. & Mrs. Tom Cavenaugh, public relations coordinator Dave Warren and a great guide, Leon Cheatom. Thanks to the entire staff of the Florida Department of Natural Resources, with special recognition to Shari Naftzinger, who is a great coordinator. I am honored to know Stewart Gregory, master instructor/instructor trainer and underwater photographer who certified me in the art of scuba diving. He made a major contribution to this book with his help and magnificent photographs on pages 11 and 152.

My photographic odyssey was complete, thanks to Rosemerry's love, and to enduring assistance from my son, Mark, including helping save my life on a river expedition.

Handmade environmental art prints are available from the author.

Technical Information

To gather the light for the images in this book, vintage 25-year-old Calumet and Plaubel view cameras were used, fitted primarily with Goertz Dagor/Artar and Schneider lenses. The time-proven Rollei SL-66 system was used for most of the wildlife images. Fujichrome professional films were selected for their ability to render color brilliance, their accurate color tonal range and their power to resolve detail. Polarizing filters were used to reduce glare and 81 series filters were used to eliminate the excessive blue spectrum.

—J.V.

Embers of golden light journey across the open Atlantic toward the Keys, north of Biscayne National Park

The fire of creation paints another day over Bahia Honda State Recreation Area, Bahia Honda Key

" . . . the sun rose from the bosom of the waters with a burst of glory that flashed on my soul the idea of that power which called into existence so magnificent an object. . . . The surface of the waters shone in its tremulous smoothness, and the deep blue of the clear heavens was pure as the world that lies beyond them." — John James Audubon